*To my muse
for existing.*

spoon full of orange peels

Criscelda Mortimore

Spoon Full of Orange Peels
Copyright 2020 Criscelda Mortimore
All rights reserved.
Book cover designed by Budi Setiawan
(IG: @boedishm)
ISBN 978-1-7356289-1-2

Table of Contents

I: And sunlight, too is good, for wounds.

Scars	2
Possibility	3
The Beautiful Unicorn	4
Swimming	5
Mouthful of Diamonds	6
The Warmth and the Light	7
Above My Midnight	8
The Present	9
Sunlight	10
Wrinkles	11
Only for You	12
A Smile	13
Lovely	14
A Room Within a Room	15
Red Roses	16
Chaste Beauty	17
Rose Petal	18
Never a Thing	19
The Mother Who Rejected Her Children	20
The Agonizing Side to Mother's Day	21
Red Butterfly	22
A Little Plastic Bag	23
Wrecked Roses	24
Wild Things	25
Marigold	26
Humility	27
The Flight of Withered Petals	28
Things	29
A Month-And-A-Half Into Quarantine	30
I Adjust My Headphones	31
Love III	32
Homeowners Insurance	33
Hedonist	34
At Last	35

```
II: I sat in a chair
and I didn't move.

I was in a dark room
and I was pleased.
```

In the Quiet	38
In a Faraway Land	39
Relief	40
Large, Black, Heavy-Duty, Industrial-Sized Trash Bags	41
For Once	42
The Sinking of a Plastic Cup	43
The Tip of My Pencil	44
Barren Walls	45
Shredded Paper	46
The Mortar and the Pestle	47
The Puzzle Is Broken	48
I Fell off the Table	49
I Gave Birth to a Son	50
Mastery of Life	51
A Poet	52
All My Best Friends	53
My Dear Friend	54
A Grey Mist	55
Just to See the Sparks	56
No	57
This Not That	58
The Experience of Dishes	59
The Little, Square, Plastic Portal	60
The L Wants to Go Somewhere	61
A Box	62
Black Stallion	63

III: I don't understand anything.

I only understand that I love you.

The One Whom Jesus Loved	66
A One Such as I	67
My Edward Scissorhands	68
In the Adoration Chapel	69
Let Me Sit Next to You	70
Conundrum	71
The Faith of Mary	72
I Tried to Be a Saint	73
What I Wish	74
Trust	75
Knowledge of Self	76
Faith II	77
Thorns	78
Try Again	80
Big White Wings	81
The Hummingbird	82
Stranger	83
Variations on a Theme	84
God and the Devil	85
Forgiveness II	86
The Holy Spirit Is	87
My Italian Father	88
In the Dark	89
Radiating Outward	90
Penance	91
Faithfulness, Gentleness	92

IV: You're so beautiful when you're eating an apple.

Preparing Basmati Rice	94
A Semi-Circle Within a Rectangle	95
Broccoli	96
My Lemon	97
The Glass Dome	98
A Blue, Plastic Cup	99
The Terrible Mistake	100
Regret	101
Butternut Squash	102
The Color of Caramel	103
The Gifts of the Blackberry	104
The Onion	105
Hot Spiced Tea	106
Cinnamon Roll	107
Blessings	108
Happiness	109
The Human Heart	110
All Things Must End	111
The Softest, Cleanest Pillow	112
Fly	113
Any More	114
Coming up for Air	115
The Void	116
Jagged Pills	117
Red Zipper	118
Cameo	119
Real People	120

**V: I am
going away
into
the dark, dark wood.**

**Never to return
again.**

I Desire Mercy, Not Sacrifice	122
I Am Trash	124
You Don't Know What Happiness Is	125
When the Birds Glide by	126
Sheets	127
The Petunias	128
The Strength of Liquid	129
Water	130
Do You Remember?	131
A Glittery Shawl	132
The Snow	133
The Once-Thought Untamable Beast	134
The Tiniest Implosion of Nothing	135
Severe Introversion	136
The Effects of Reading Simone Weil	137
The Armenian Genocide	138
Pride and Envy	139
I Pray for You	140
Young vs. Old	141
The Runt	142
The Passing of Time	143
The Flight of the Bunny Rabbit	144
A Moment in the Life of a 39-Year-Old Woman	145
Tramp Stamp	146
Addiction	147
A Good Reason to Keep Living	148
A Wispy Little Creature	149
Life	150

I: And sunlight, too
is good, for wounds.

Scars

I
didn't want you
to feel pain.

But pain
can shape us
into something better
something higher
something
much more beautiful

though covered with scars.

Possibility

You could be so much better.
If only
you left those toxic people.
If only
you had more sunlight.
If only
your person
would love you
as they ought.

The Beautiful Unicorn

The beautiful unicorn
comes to me
in the glen.

His white mane
hangs down
his golden horn
glimmers.

The beautiful unicorn
has finally come
to trust me
and allow me to be near.

I cherish this beast.
And so
I only look

grateful
for every second
my eyes
can lay upon him.

I only look.
I keep my hands
clasped
behind my back.

Swimming

I would like to go swimming.
I would like to be
alone
in the water.
I would like to feel
the water
touching
my entire body
caressing me
massaging me.

I would like to hear
nothing
but the dull roar
of the water
sloshing
against my ears.

I would like to feel
my body
wet
and tired
and energized
as I pull myself
from the water
and head
to the shower.

Mouthful of Diamonds

Riding
in my car
top down
music up
wind
in my hair.

The Warmth and the Light

You make me feel joy
I didn't know there was still
so much left
in this broken body

Light your fire
your fire
lights mine
my fire
lights yours

we all need the warmth
and the light

Above My Midnight

I wonder about you.
Where are your footsteps falling now?
Who are you making smile now?

I like
simply knowing
that you exist.

Your light
like dawn
rising
above my midnight.

The Present

I
gave you
a present.

It was small.
It was homemade.
It was
in a junky
Christmas bag
though it was September

have I ever seen?
Anything?
More beautiful?
Than your humble smile?
Than your joy?
At receiving something
so very
small?

Sunlight

I've been stripped of everything.
But I saw you today
and
even in my poverty
even in my leprosy
I was granted
sunlight.

Wrinkles

I love
every single wrinkle
on your beautiful
face.

Only for You

I smiled at you.
And you
smiled at me.
And that
was all that mattered.

A Smile

A smile
communicates
so much.

An upturned
corner
of a mouth

A life force
paused.
Taking in.
Gaining pleasure.

Lovely

How lovely
to see you
and smile
and feel light.

A Room Within a Room

There is a room.
Enter that room.
See what a privilege!
To be in such
a restricted space.

And here
together
we live
in that room.

Then
one day
you discover
upon pulling
a book
off the shelf

that there is
another room
a smaller room
a room
within a room
deep
deep
within.

Red Roses

In a defenseless place I sit and wait
to go confess and as the priest walks past
exquisite scent, a pure enchanting state
four walls of roses, stacked and tightly packed.

Seductive flower, lush and deep, dark red
with petals soft and velvet as doeskin
mesmeric swirl of beauty coveted
that hypnotizes, leads to falling in.

O outward symbol shameless and exposed
that represents her secret dark and deep
a duty-laden grant within the folds
in our time, lost respect and lost mystique.

At once, good things in her which make you stay
and also that which carries you away.

Chaste Beauty

She sits
beneath the cherry blossom tree.
The thick
white petals
descend
upon her
slowly.

Rose Petal

I found
a rose petal.

Pale pink
at the curve
pale yellow
at the point

run through
with veins

soft
and velvety
and waiting
to be crushed.

Never a Thing

Never a thing
more beautiful and pure
than you.

Never a thing
more delectable and tender
than you.

The Mother Who Rejected Her Children

The snow is piled up
and dirty.
And
covered
with broken, musty brown leaves.

Why?
Because
they flew
from a nearby tree
who refused to feed them
anymore.

Preferring
to be alone
preferring
to be bare.

And now
the tree still lives
while the leaves
moulder.

The Agonizing Side to Mother's Day

A mother and a daughter, thirty seven
though many years apart, age, parallel
the daughter's life, it seems, has become heaven
the mother, at that age, was living hell.

The daughter does not worry over food
she spills her feelings to her therapist
the mother, she was homeless with her brood
those she could lean on, empty was the list.

It seems that life's a pitiless hand-dealer
to some she gives a good hand, others, bad
my mom, it seems, there's nothing that can heal her
she breaks all, and for this I'm always sad.

Unnatural, yet it's best to stay away
the agonizing side to Mother's Day.

Red Butterfly

What is this red butterfly?
That I found
on the floor?

It is a toy.
Brought into my life
because
I had children.

It is plastic.
Like
so many things
in my life.

It is
a lego
a piece
meant to be added
to many other pieces

I lament
red butterfly
help me
find a reason
to rejoice.

A Little Plastic Bag

I packed you
a little yogurt
all my love
was in that yogurt.

Edges
carefully wiped clean
a spoon
conscientiously packed along

all
in a little plastic bag
in a little plastic bag.

Wrecked Roses

Sunshine
brought me roses.

Yellow ones
and
pale pink ones.

My children
wrecked them
petals
scattered.

The petals
dried
and
my!
how beautiful!
they remain.

Wild Things

I opened up my life.

To let it bleed.

I watch beauty
and grace
from afar

while chaos
smashes around me

while chaos
crawls on all fours

and brings wild things
all around me.

Marigold

A humble marigold in a wee pot
delights a mother and her children who
all went together to the flower shop
entombed the seeds 'till green came into view.

Across the ocean people gather to
take pleasure in the Gardens of Versailles
much pomp and throngs of fans they have accrued
their great laudation does not uglify
the richness in that tiny universe
where something small allows it's glory meek
to radiate itself out and traverse
between the planets, so that it may cleave
itself unto the minds of those, though few
who find fulfillment in the miniscule.

Humility

Humility
is
becoming nothing
and being glad for it.

Humility
moves
to the side
and smiles
while others shine.

Humility
is like
having an old
tattered cloak
for skin.

The Flight of Withered Petals

There are
little
withered
yellow petals
scattered all over the floor.

Gathering
the petals
one by one

they animate
and take flight
lifting off
and away
from my hands.

Things

The world
is full
of so many things.

I couldn't possibly
manage it all.

I couldn't possibly
rescue it all.

I couldn't possibly
salvage it all.

I think
I will let it all
slip
through my fingers
instead.

A Month-And-A-Half Into Quarantine

I forgot about you
it wasn't hard to do.

I collapsed
inward
on myself.

It was bound to happen.

I Adjust My Headphones

I adjust my headphones
so that the drug
can be injected
directly
into my brain.

Love III

I love this couch.
And this couch
loves me.

I lie
in it's embrace
all day!

And
all day
it embraces
me.

Homeowners Insurance

I don't want to think
about
homeowners insurance.

Liabilities
Deductibles
misfortunes
protecting myself
against
humanity's ugliness.

I'd rather think about
my black dress
blowing
in the wind

your lovely face
smiling at me

the way it felt
when everything
was
as it should have been.

Hedonist

If left
to my own
devices.

If freed
from the burden
of expectations.

I would
fill my belly
with peanut butter cookies
and lay in my bed
in the middle
of the day.

At Last

Here I am
in my bed
at last.

II: I sat in a chair
and I didn't move.

I was in a dark room
and I was pleased.

In the Quiet

In the quiet
my pencil
moves
through the air
like
a sledgehammer
falling
in slow motion
the air
thick as cream
waiting
to be whipped
into a thick
froth.

In a Faraway Land

In a faraway land
I open the refrigerator door.

The world
is in panic
around me.

Should I
call my mother?

Should I?
Try to run back?

No.
If I die
it will be here.
In my faraway land
in my separateness.

In my faraway land
I open the refrigerator door
my bare feet
against the linoleum floor.

Relief

I took
all the plates
out of the cupboard.
And all of the dirty ones
out of the kitchen sink.

I hauled
my tub
of plates
to the cliff
where I run away.

Standing
looking over the edge
I dumped them all!
And down they went!
And they all
shattered.

I went home.
To an empty sink.
And an empty cupboard.
And felt relief.

Large, Black, Heavy-Duty, Industrial-Sized Trash Bags

I took
all
of my hatred
and all
of my resentment
and piled it
into four, large, black, heavy-duty
industrial-sized
trash bags.
They are sitting in my garage.
As soon
as I am able
I will take them
to the dump.

For Once

I hold two glass jars
in my hands.

And
for once
I don't restrain myself.

I take those two glass jars
like
a pair of cymbals
and crash!
and smash!
them together.

Of course
the pieces
slice into my hands
of course
there is blood
everywhere.

Of course
it hurts
and
I will have to go
to the emergency room.

But
I'm still glad
I still
feel gratified
that I didn't restrain myself
for once.

The Sinking of a Plastic Cup

I watched
the red plastic bottle
fill
and fill
with water.

It rocked
back and forth
resisting
but
the more it resisted
the more
it filled with water.

Now
it lies
alone
at the bottom
of the dirty sink

Bits
of debris
floating
all around

in the stillness
in the quiet
in the bottom
of the sink.

The Tip of My Pencil

The tip of my pencil
is so sharp.

The tip
of my pencil
such a lovely
little cone.

The tip of my pencil
could pierce right through.

Barren Walls

The walls in here are white.
The walls in here
are bare.

They go
on and on
like a great
blank
sheet of paper.

Like someone
has taken
a giant eraser
and erased
everything
I put there.

Shredded Paper

There is
a plastic bag
full of shredded paper.

The papers
perfectly cut
thin strips

are a ghost
of what they once were.

Words, paragraphs
once relaying a message
now
unrecognizable fractals of words
letters
cut in half

the message
taken
from their mouths.

The Mortar and the Pestle

I
pick up
the mortar
and
the pestle.

They are
very heavy
in my hands.

Such
heavy stone
can crush you.

Indeed
it was made
to crush.

I pick up
my mortar and pestle

I make peace
with it's hardness
with it's
complete lack

of mercy.

The Puzzle Is Broken

The puzzle
is broken.

The pieces
are scattered

I turn over
each piece
one by one.

The puzzle
is broken.

I Fell off the Table

I
fell
off the table.

I
drank too much
danced
too much
laughed
too much.

You
had to catch me
at the bottom.
You
had to hold my head
as I laughed
and gazed
at the stars.

I Gave Birth to a Son

I gave birth to a son.
And he keeps me
tethered to this world.

Light from darkness.
Happiness from sadness.
Boundless energy
from
something tired.

Something
that belongs
from something
that does not.

Mastery of Life

I've been here
for so long.

I've seen
so much.

And still
still
I understand
so little.

A Poet

A poet is always on the outside
observing
through a pane of glass.

A poet
always sits
at a table
alone.

A poet
is helpless
before her poems
limp.

Her face
falls
downward

as she sits
inside her mind
peering out.

All My Best Friends

All my best friends are dead.
And they are far more reliable
than the living ones.

We cavort
in my room
alone.

How lively they are!
How absolutely
alive.

My Dear Friend

My dear friend.

I look
upon your face
as we are suspended
underwater.

All around me
it is blue!
And your porcelain skin
so beautiful
how my heart
bursts with love
for you.

A Grey Mist

Since when?
Does grey?
Have to be?
Sad?
Depressing?
Blah?

Maybe I twirl
maybe I swirl around
in a grey mist

where I belong.

Maybe there
I feel good.

Maybe there
I open my palm
and let all of you go
let all of you
disappear
into the mist.

Just to See the Sparks

On the Fourth of July
in Budapest
a priest
misses the fireworks.

He sits
alone
on a hotel room floor
and strikes matches
just
to see
the sparks.

No

The word "no"
so short.
A tiny door
which opens
and sucks everything into it
then slams shut.

and you
left
on the outside
of the tiny door
now sealed shut.

Your hands
empty
the air around you
empty.

This Not That

I can't do that
but I can do this.

I can't
play the keys
make the melody
in my mind
come
out of my fingers
with mastery
with precision

but I can do this
I can
pound
I can
whisper
I can
carve with precision
words
onto paper.

The Experience of Dishes

What dishes must feel
soaking in the sink
their grime
slowly sinking to the bottom

nestling
against each other
tangled together
instead of neatly stacked
each one
to his appropriate cupboard

the gorgeous suds
surrounding them
all
after having done
their duty.

The Little, Square, Plastic Portal

I found
a little
clear
plastic
square
on the floor

Turns out
you can put your finger through it
and poke your finger
into another dimension

somewhere
in another dimension
your finger
is poking through.

The L Wants to Go Somewhere

The L wants to go somewhere.
It curves up, then falls downward
then loops again
and presses forward.

Forward
toward something…
Love? Perhaps?
Lilies? Maybe?
Listen…

A Box

I
wanted
to fit
into a box.

A box!
with it's
comforting
confining sides!

A box
a safe little place
to hide.

Alas.
I shall never
ever
fit.

I may as well
make the best
of it.

Black Stallion

The horses that are in the stable, kept
have traded wild freedom for their care
not like Black Stallion, who will not accept
the bridle as his mane whips in the air.

'Tis only right, Black Stallion ought be free
'Tis only right, Black Stallion ought be fierce
these qualities of authenticity
they benefit as much as they do pierce.

'Tis treacherous to always be alone
with no one there to help you if you fall
but you will find your true self, overthrown
if you let them lead you into the stall.

So singular, creating wind, unlashed
Black Stallion running through the mountains, fast.

III: I don't understand anything.

I only understand that I love you.

The One Whom Jesus Loved

Oh
to be
the one whom Jesus loved.

oh
to recline
at his side.

oh
to lean back
against his chest
and
looking up
into his eyes
to ask
(as a child
asks a mother)
"Master, who is it?"

A One Such as I

Jesus.
You make me uncomfortable.
Though I love you so.

Why?
Must we go?
to places
so unpleasant?

I am not a fitting companion for you.
I love comfort!
I love
to feel good.

What a strange mystery
that a one
such as I
would love you.

that a one
such as I
would follow after you at all.

My Edward Scissorhands

Yes.
You are the one.
My only one.

My Edward Scissorhands.
My inquisitor.
You hang me
upside-down
naked.
You humiliate me
You cut me
with your caresses.

But yes.
You are the one.
The only one.

In the Adoration Chapel

When I moved
in the adoration chapel
my shoes
were too noisy.

Every step
a clumsy
loud
awkward
squeak
against the perfectly polished
high-gloss
tiled
floor.

Let Me Sit Next to You

Let me sit next to you.
at least.

I've had your platter
piled with humiliation
and thorns
I am not so naïve
as to beg for whatever you have
to give me
anymore.

But still
I'd like to sit next to you.
I don't know what to say.
I have nothing to say.
But let my energy
touch yours.

For I cannot leave you!
I cannot
forget you.
I cannot
eat what you serve
I'm not strong enough
not good enough
not noble enough
not
holy
enough.

Nor do I even wish to be holy.
But
I cannot leave you
and I cannot forget you.
So please
just let me sit next to you.

Amen.

Conundrum

We sit together
You and I
I look at You
You
look at me.

Remember?
When I laid my head?
Upon Your chest?

And now?
A great chasm
between us.

I just
really don't understand
why You did what You did.

I look at it
and I see
pieces
that just don't fit together

that could've been whole
that could've been better spent.

Was it me?
Did I hear you wrong?
Am I insane?

Oh.
But You
are all good
    all loving
    all powerful

and here

the conundrum.

The Faith of Mary

What is
the faith
of Mary?

It is
seeing your
perfect, beautiful
son
hanging
shredded

It is
being unable
to heal him
with your hands
with your embrace
and saying

God
I trust you.

I Tried to Be a Saint

I tried to be a saint.

That is to say
I tried to forget about myself.
I could not.

I tried to be a saint.
That is to say
I tried to emanate joy.
I did not.

I tried.
I tried.
I tried to love.
But
my heart was barren.

I tried.
I tried.
I…

What I Wish

The kind
of courage
you require of me

I do not wish to have.

I do not wish
to embrace death.

I do not wish
to love someone
so much more than myself.

I do not wish
to trust you
so deeply
that I sleep
soundly
in the middle
of a storm.

What I do wish
is to scuttle about
in darkness
like a cockroach.

Scuttling
soundlessly
behind the walls.
My exoskeleton
of fear
protecting me
keeping me alive
for billions of years
always
to scuttle
in the darkness.

Trust

She sits
and looks out the window

there's nothing to fear
in her world
she knows so little yet

She is a child
and she sits
as a child
in complete trust
for wherever
I may take her.

Knowledge of Self

I don't want to know myself.

I
don't want
to look
at myself.
I don't want
to think
about myself.

It causes me
to squirm.

Faith II

I
have faith
in the ether.

I have faith
in the clear blue

in the scarlet passion
of dancing bodies.

I have faith in my respect
and awe
for beauty.

I will care for it
even
when I care nothing
for myself.

Thorns

"I'm all thorns"
He says to me
"Can you handle it?"
"No"
I reply
"I cannot.

Thorns?!
That was never what I wanted.
What I wanted
was your embrace."
"The thorns"
He said
"are the way
to freedom.
Do you wish to be free?"
"Of course I do!
Of course I do."
I replied.

"You must
be out of those chains
to embrace me."

Then He looked at me
and smiled
so tenderly.

I thought about it
and replied
"I don't like that.
Why?
Why must there be thorns?
To get to You?
Why can't?
It all be
pleasure pleasure pleasure?
You love me?
Why can't you give me?
Nothing
but pleasure?"

And as the words
fell
from my mouth
I knew
that
was a ridiculous question
from a ridiculous, albeit beloved
person.

Try Again

Raise your eyes
to the mountains
breathe
deeply
the clean air

try again
today
to consider
the idea
that you
are not
trash

that you
just might
have value

infinite value
even.

Big White Wings

Why
can't you come
and enfold me.

Place your
big
white wings around me.

Make sure
nothing comes in.

Make sure
I never leave.

The Hummingbird

Thank you
for the moment
when
a hummingbird
and I
came face to face.

He hovered
inches from my face
wings
buzzing

such a small
marvelous thing
completely lacking
fear

ready
and armed
with
a long needle
beak.

Stranger

I'm always here
with me.

I often speak
of myself.

I glance
into the mirror
and there
my face
the same face
always
glances back.

And
somehow
after
all this

Still.
I know not
myself.

Variations on a Theme

It wouldn't matter
who you were thinking of
in that moment.

Anyone
Anything
that you run away with
still causes you to leave.

It wouldn't matter
what
you place on top.
If it were in the wrong order
It is still
in the wrong order.

That
is why
we are all
variations
on a theme.

God and the Devil

God
is very
efficient
with His words.

The devil
is not.

Forgiveness II

To forgive
is
to take an eraser
and smudge.

The Holy Spirit Is

The Holy Spirit is unicorns
purple horns and sparkling manes
prancing
absolutely everywhere.

The Holy Spirit is mammoth marshmallows
with golden horns and ears
filling up the room
the mirth of children.

The Holy Spirit
is everywhere
carelessly tossed on the counter
displayed in the grocery store
resting on the head
of a little child.

My Italian Father

Padre
my Italian father
waves his hand to the right
and the demons flee.

In the Dark

I look at you.
Across the way.
In the dark.

I haven't
been able to see you.

I haven't
been able to be one with you
alone with you
consuming you.

But
I now know
as I look across the room
in the dark
that you haven't forgotten me
that your love for me
is far more beautiful
than my love for you.

Radiating Outward

I just really miss you.
Nothing will fall into place
until I can be with you.
My desire for you
is
ever present
always

always
radiating
outward.

Penance

My mind
is dirty water
swishing
swirling
thrashing.

Come
and set your feet upon my mind.
Make the water clean.
Make the water still.

Amen

Faithfulness, Gentleness

I'm faithful to grind this pepper.
I'm faithful to take these steps
in the hot sun.

I'm faithful
to lie here in the dark
and shut my eyes.

I'm faithful
to ride this bicycle.

I'll be gentle
when I've accomplished
exactly nothing
when
I knock everything over
when my greatest accomplishment
is lying on the couch
because it means
I haven't run away.

IV: You're so beautiful
when you're eating an apple.

Preparing Basmati Rice

My hand
swirling
in the water.

The rice
soft
beneath my fingers.

Swirl.
Round and round
and round
and round.

A Semi-Circle Within a Rectangle

Grapefruit!
Inside a plastic container.

It's orange
tinted
with pink.

The tupperware
clear
with black handles.

I'll put it in the fridge

a semi-circle
within a rectangle.

Broccoli

Broccoli.

Vivid green.

Steaming
off my fork.

Broccoli

chlorophyll fronds
tender bite
creamy and woodsy and warm.

My Lemon

I smelled you
my lemon

I felt you
my lemon
close
to my lips

cold
and filling my mouth
with fragrance.

The Glass Dome

There was a glass dome.
I put my fingers
upon it
and caressed it.
 so smooth
 and clear
 and elegant

he
picked up the glass dome
and gingerly
set it to the side

wanting
the cake inside
wanting
the sauce
which was pooled
at the base.

A Blue, Plastic Cup

I picked up
a blue, plastic
cup

The light
passed through
the blue plastic
cup

at the bottom
of the cup
a tiny ocean
rocked
back and forth

on that
tiny ocean
in the sun
I rock
back and forth
lazily.

The Terrible Mistake

I went
to The Cheesecake Factory
(I had a gift certificate.)

I thought
I'll just get
a slice of cheesecake!
Why not?
Every now and then.

I went home
and thought
I wonder
how many calories?
in that
one slice
of cheesecake?

I found
the answer.
1500!!!
1500 calories!
In one
single
slice
of cheesecake.

What had I done?
It was
as if
I'd slept with a hooker
and gotten an STD.
A terrible mistake
that will stay
and stay
and stay…

Regret

I
deeply
deeply
regret
that
I won't
be able
to consume
this mac n' cheese
with it's tender pasta
with it's creamy sauce
with it's
sweet
firm peas
that pop
in your mouth.

Butternut Squash

I'm peeling a butternut squash.

The thin skin
emerges
between the blades
of my vegetable peeler.

The squash
has this lovely shape
slim on top
round
on the bottom
but
it makes it hard to peel.

The peels
thin
mellow yellow
on one side
tan
on the other
are even lovely
in their pile.

My peeler
has a hard time
grasping the skin
but
when she is all done
when
she is stripped naked
how beautiful!

The Color of Caramel

This tea
is the color
of caramel.

This spoon
so long and silver.

My teapot
heavy and black.

This tea
the color of caramel.

The Gifts of the Blackberry

Is there anything more beautiful?
Than a blackberry?

Is there anything more?
Filled with black luscious juice?

How it shines.
How
it is a thing
clustered
but still

one.

How it's seeds
remain
in my teeth

long after
I have inhaled the rest
giving me something
to chew.

The Onion

Knife edge
plunging
through an onion.

The flesh
parts
before the blade

the blade
slides through
'till
the bottom
is struck.

Hot Spiced Tea

I remember
you had
two cups
of hot spiced tea.

And I
wanting to be closer
to you
followed suit.

Cinnamon Roll

I
was given
a very large
sweet
rich
soft
cinnamon roll.

I carried it around with me.
And, every once in a while
I looked around
and, making sure I was alone
I sunk my teeth
into it.

It is soft
it is sweet
it is bready
it is creamy

and it is rich
in my mouth.

Blessings

What
a blessing
this tea
this
sweater
these
wool socks.

What
a blessing
this
breathing
in and out
this
eye contact
with
another human.

What a beauty!
This
sweet potato bread
with it's warm orange.

What a wonder
this blurting out
of my love
in a moment
of weakness.

Happiness

Happiness is
an everything bagel.

It's toasted
and it crunches
in my mouth
as I look out the window.

I'm in a scrubby café
on a cool Colorado morning
alone
observing
all the beautiful people

all the beautiful
beautiful
people.

The Human Heart

I
had the pantry
all organized
but still
everything fell apart.

I set out
all the breakfast items
but still
everything fell apart.

The human heart
doesn't have enough
to carry us through.

The human heart
is so abundant
with rich beauty.

All Things Must End

The arm
on my chair
is threadbare.

I place my finger
beneath the fraying thread

I get the feeling
that this chair
may not be around
much longer

after all
all things
must end
no?

The Softest, Cleanest Pillow

The lie
was comforting
the lie
was warm.

Like
the softest, cleanest
pillow.

I rested my head
upon it.

But
my head fell through
and underneath
a black
dusty
hollow.

I fell in.
I scrambled
for my pillow!
For my soft! and clean!

Someone like me
will never have a pillow.
It simply
wasn't meant to be.

Fly

There's a fly in the house.
His thick, filthy body
thuds…
thud
thud
thud
against the windowpane.

He buzzes
and buzzes
the buzz
sinking
into
my
brain.

Any More

I don't even care anymore.
I ate fried chicken, with a side of cold french fries
dipped in
cheese gravy
for lunch.

I
don't
even
care anymore.

My t-shirt is too tight
I don't even try to suck in my gut.

I don't
even care
any more.

Coming up for Air

My head.
Out.
of my phone.

Feels like.
Coming up for air.

The Void

I like
touching this box of cereal.

I like
peering into the cupboard.

I like
the way my pencil
slides
across this paper
upon this shelf.

I like
forgetting
about everyone
on social media

that cupboard
which opens
into a void
a deep
endless
frivolous
void.

Jagged Pills

I tried
to swallow those pills
but
they were just
too jagged
they were just
too big
they got caught
in my throat.

Red Zipper

I grabbed
the red zipper
and pulled
upwards.

Cameo

I walked into your shop
I remember it so vividly.

I pushed my stroller
through your doors
you were kind to my children.

I gave you my cameo
to clean
and when you returned it to me
I was astonished.

Someone
who?
I will never know
cleaned it.
With worshipful care.
It was
simply radiant.

It was
something
in my dirty life
that was
perfectly
radiant

though still
with a crack.

Real People

real people are fat.
they are
terribly
imperfect.

real people
are old
and young
their faces
covered with crumbs.

real people
can smile
at one another
across the table
and not care
that they are fat
that they are old
that their faces
are covered

with crumbs.

V: I am
going away
into
the dark, dark wood.

Never to return
again.

I Desire Mercy, Not Sacrifice

I go to mass
every Sunday.

I cover my head
I bow
before
the precious Eucharist.

I struggle with my children
"Let's go see Jesus"
I say.

I reverently walk up
to receive
hands folded
opening my mouth wide
eager
for His body
and His blood.

I chew the host
and drink
the cup
and I feel
so grateful.

Yesterday
Jesus came to my window.

Unexpected.
Black.
Physically
and mentally
handicapped.

My curtains
were drawn.

I hesitated.
I considered
hiding.

I eventually let Him in.
Begrudgingly.
He sat
on my sofa
watching us eat.
His exposed mouth
filled
with sharp and colliding teeth
made me lose
my appetite.

I sought
for ways
to make Him leave.

I gave him
a glass of water
not wanting
His fingers
to touch mine.

And when
He finally left
I was relieved.

I Am Trash

I
am
trash.

I
lie
on
the bottom
of the
wastebasket.

I am
unattractive.

Unwanted.

I lie
on
the
bottom
of
the
wastebasket.

What more can I do?

You Don't Know What Happiness Is

You don't know what happiness is.
Because
it is absence.
Because
it is ignorance.
Because
not wanting it
not seeking it
not even
pondering it
means
you have it.

When the Birds Glide by

What does it mean?
When the birds fly by?

The passing of time
The passing of desires.

What does it mean?
When the birds glide by?

Sheets

I bought those sheets
long ago.

They were on clearance
it was winter.

The sheets
are light
and thin
and make you think
of a summer house.

Winter is gone.
Summer has arrived
once again.

And the sheets
the sheets
make you dream
of a house
on the lake
in the summer.

The Petunias

The petunias are dead.
How resilient they were!
They bloomed in the summer
resplendent.
Bursting with fresh color while the other flowers
died
in the hot sun
withered
and charred.
But now
the snow
has fallen
upon them…
Who knows?
They might survive
even this.

The Strength of Liquid

water
pouring
from a glass bottle.

liquid clear
pouring
from hard clear.

liquid
pouring
over glass.

liquid
pouring into glass

seeming
to conform

seeming to
take it's shape

but really

it's only
waiting

for the chance
to flow.

Water

The flowers
drink it.

I drink it.

Water cleanses us.

Water kills us.

Water
most monstrous
carrying
the monsters
most frightening
in her
dark
unknowable
black
womb.

Do You Remember?

Do you remember how it felt?
Last summer?
When the parking lot
was so full?
And the rain was pouring down?
And everything
was so gray?
And the puddles
drenched your feet
And
you had to run?

A Glittery Shawl

I took a shower.
The hot water
cascaded
down my back
a glittery shawl.

The Snow

The snow
jets down
piling fast
nothing
can stop
it's relentless drive
it will overtake
one tiny
feeble
snowflake
at a time.

The Once-Thought Untamable Beast

air
dries things
presses us
to the earth.

air
can be sliced through
harnessed
we
can
place a metal saddle
upon it
and ride it.

air
the once-thought
untamable
beast.

The Tiniest Implosion of Nothing

I
swallowed
a galaxy.

In it went
with it's black space
and it's glittering stars

with it's
black holes
and comets.

In it went
a vast thing
folded up
again
and again
until
it imploded

The tiniest implosion
of nothing.

Severe Introversion

I
have a headache
and
I am depleted
from
so much
human interaction.

The Effects of Reading Simone Weil

I placed a peach
upon a plate
effortlessly
nimble
a quick step
from my hand
to the plate
it's skin
still wet
from it's quick rinse

Simone
don't make me lose sleep
again
tonight.

You say
it is natural
for men to murder

at least I have this peach.

> *My own feeling was that once a certain class of people has been placed [...] outside the ranks of those whose life has value, then nothing comes more naturally to men than murder. As soon as men know that they can kill without fear of punishment or blame, they kill; or at least they encourage killers with approving smiles.*
>
> *Simone Weil*
> *Letter to Georges Bernanos*

The Armenian Genocide

"Armenians we shall exterminate."
The Empire Ottoman formed a cabal.
"If leader or a sage, eradicate!"
Methodic and thought-through their rationale.

Step one: Remove protection. Kill their men.
Step two: Women and children. Make them march.
We'll rape and rob and brutalize again
by forcing them to watch their children starve.

A group, it seemed, that God had cast aside.
Today, their bones abandoned in Deir Ez-Zor.
Atrocity! It leaves me terrified!
Our cruelty laid bare in a time of war.

And yet, somehow, their faith, it was not wrecked!
Such hope, within me, it doth resurrect.

Pride and Envy

She looms and seeks to rule with many eyes
a calculating, cunning, shining spider
you'll see that she is Pride, once undisguised
and over time there's no one could abide her.

How strange that she should draw that sniveling weakling
Envy, her name, forever discontent
her problems with you only faced obliquely
her value only by diminishment
of others who have things that she does not
although if she would only look around
she'd see that she has really got a lot
and jealousy has truly got her bound

Although from these two types most would take flight
disdain gave them a reason to unite.

I Pray for You

I pray for you
you
who wounded me
so long ago.

It still hurts
my tears
still spill.

But
I offer them up
for you.

Know this.
In wounding me
you have gained.

I will pray for you.
Every time I remember.
Every time I cry.
Every time I despair.
I will pray for you.

In this way
we are bonded
together
for all eternity.

Young vs. Old

The old
swaddle themselves
with
comforting lies.

The young
rip off
the lies
with abandoned glee.

The Runt

The runt
of the litter
is small
he is hungry

he is
not pretty.

The runt
starves
and
is isolated

his jock brethren
pile
upon the latest kill.

The runt
slowly starves
and
after his life
of misery
is over

his mother
and
his brethren
tear the runt
apart.

The Passing of Time

Already.
This moment
was
a long time ago.

The Flight of the Bunny Rabbit

a child
sits
cross-legged
in the grass.

a large
stuffed
boa constrictor
wrapped
around her waist

to her left
a bunny rabbit
flees.

A Moment in the Life of a 39-Year-Old Woman

It's cold outside.
The curtain
rustles
against the screen.

Not far away
a train
sounds
it's alarm.

And I sit here
growing older
and older…

Tramp Stamp

Young
and beautiful
'twas something
to behold.

Old
and flabby
I
am now
a
joke.

May I be
the one
who laughs
hardest.

May I
grab the knife
of humiliation
and relish
the cut.

Addiction

I remember
the way you smelled.

Your smoke
wafting past
my nose
heavy smoke
filling my lungs

I sat on the back porch
your
beautiful glow
between my fingers

and the sky!
so black
and so filled
with stars.

A Good Reason to Keep Living

But You love me?
Then
I can keep going.

A Wispy Little Creature

Hope
is a wispy little creature
who
for all his
nothingness
is
remarkably strong.

Just when
you thought
that he was buried
beneath that pile of dead leaves
he lifts his head.

Life

I heard you screaming
against the grey sky.

The screams
were like
a shotgun
in a place of quiet.

I felt your
oblivious joy
against our collective apprehension

Such a wild, untamable, unstoppable thing

life.

The End

www.ingramcontent.com/pod-product-compliance
Lightning Source LLC
Chambersburg PA
CBHW020908080526
44589CB00011B/496